Something To Chew On

The day was dawning. Millions of snowflakes were falling from the glowing sky onto the awakening small town, whose dwellers were eagerly awaiting Christmas and their Christmas Fayre.

The Christmas Fayre holds out the promise of a number of interesting activities for visitors. There is, for example, the cake contest, which had already begun in the early morning. The furry paws of the excited contestants were eager to get to work.

The tiny wooden houses and bakeries were filled with dozens of bags of flour. Gingerbread was being baked in one place, chimney cake in the second, and muffins decorated with chocolate icing in the third. The smell of steaming freshly baked bread and fluffy buttery scones wafted out of the opened windows of the bakeries, along with the mouth-watering aromas of vanilla, orange zest and cinnamon.

The dense winter fog descended slowly and softly, and shrouded the small town, as if it had suddenly felt the temptation to take a closer look at the delicacies that were being prepared. It sneaked cautiously toward the cottages, blended with the heady scent of the delicacies for a moment, then gracefully drifted away toward the homes of the sleeping dwellers, to awaken them to the long-awaited day.

Meanwhile, Peter Vole, the organiser of the cake contest, was twiddling his little fingers nervously, and tapping his foot.

'What if I tasted one of the cakes unnoticed? I am so tremendously hungry! I would just sneak in there, as if I was checking something. Anyway, no one would notice!' he thought to himself.

In one of the wooden huts an almond pie was baking in the beehive oven while another was cooling on the window sill. A small pine twig was laid on each slice to decorate it. He peeped through the open window.

"Is this ornament edible? Is it made of marzipan?" he asked himself.

However, his hunger allowed no delay. He picked up one of the almond pie slices with his small paw and stuffed it into his mouth. But he soon regretted his act when he realised that the pine twig wasn't made of marzipan. He was just trying to take out of his mouth, when he heard a familiar voice behind his back.

"Good morning, Mr Vole," said the owner of the voice, and patted him on the back in greeting so hard that he almost choked. "How is the work going?"

"Oh, Mr. Mayor! What a thurprithe!" mumbled Peter Vole with a lisp from trying to hide the prickly ornament in one of his cheek pouches.

"Are you all right? Half of your face looks swollen. Is there a problem with your teeth? You can't appear on stage in such a state. Please, Mr Vole, pull yourself together!"

Peter was dripping sweat, he was so nervous. When the mayor left him alone, he was trembling as he snatched the pine twig out of his mouth. It had caused him enormous pain and pricked his cheek pouch so much that he couldn't eat anything. He just spent the rest of the morning lethargically mooching around the town as if he had done something useful.

But his mooching around caught someone's eye. This was Samson Mouse, Peter's best friend. The confident and elegant Samson had tried countless times to help smooth his little clumsy friend's ways, with varying success. He knew that Peter was a smart and decent vole, so he decided to support him in everything patiently and constantly.

The little mouse's tiny button eyes stared at Peter. He couldn't pass by without saying a word.

"Peter, why are you wandering aimlessly? What's wrong with you again?" he screamed at him. Peter froze.

"With me? Nothing. I am just checking the... the cakes."

"Is your speech ready for the public event? You know that the mayor is counting on you!" said the little mouse firmly.

While Samson scolded Peter, someone else was working hard in a small room near the main square. Cecily Clumsy was late. She would have been one of the participants in the competition, but Ms Clumsy did nothing but wail and rush about. And, of course, she was continuously given to curtsying to everyone in a kind of hesitant way.

Before leaving, she had put on her thick glasses, admiring her reflection in the mirror with satisfaction. She stepped into her new black stilettos, tottered to the clothes rack, and slipped on her fur coat. It was fluffy and protected Cecily's rounded body perfectly from the cold, so she walked out into the frosty, slippery street confidently.

Although it was late in the morning, the view over the small town was still obscured by a veil of mist which didn't want to drift away. But the dwellers of the small town didn't seem at all bothered by it. An army of squeaking mice was skating or building snowmen. The treats and hot drinks helped them to forget about the fog, which had made them feel drowsy in the morning.

Cecily Clumsy teetered along the streets in her new high-heeled shoes. With her tiny feet, she was trying to walk elegantly towards the bakery, when a badly aimed snowball hit her in the head. The accident was compounded by a sledge racing straight toward her. The trudging lady mouse was knocked over onto her back. When she fell over her glasses fogged up, and her head got trapped in her fur coat.

After five minutes of tossing and turning on the ground, she was still unable to escape from her coat.

"Please wait, Ms Cecily, I will help you. Believe me, patience is at the core of everything, so try to calm down," said Samson Mouse calmly. In the blink of an eye, he solved the problem. He loosened the stuck coat zipper with some olive oil hand cream, and gently untangled the coat from Cecily's head.

"Well, what a gentleman you are!" Cecily Clumsy sighed thankfully, still trembling.

"Peter!" Samson turned towards Peter. "As I can see, poor Ms Cecily is late. What if you made yourself useful? You should help her!"

"Great idea, my dear friend. I couldn't have said it better myself!" replied the panic-stricken Peter.

The old lady gazed up at the face of her new helper with sparkling eyes and hooked her arm through his gingerly. Cecily was happy to stroll around the streets of the town on Peter's right arm.

But as she entered the bakery, Cecily became anxious again, so Peter decided to take matters into his own hands.

"Ms Cecily, please, don't panic! Believe me, it never leads to a good outcome. Let me see! What would you like to bake?"

"Oh, alas! My gracious mouse whiskers! I have no idea! There are so many options!"

"Don't you know? I thought you had already decided a long time ago!"

She spluttered thousands of reasons for why improvisation seemed a much better idea, and anyway her decision to take part in the completion was spontaneous.

'What a fortunate thing it was that Cecily wasn't the baker, just the owner of the bakery. Otherwise, the whole town would have starved to death!' Peter thought with a sigh. Quick as lightning, he got to work.

While baking, his morning accident with the pine twigs came into his mind.

"Ms Cecily, would you be so kind as to fetch some red, green and brown marzipan? Can you manage this?"

"Of course. But why do you need the marzipan? And what should we name the cake?"

"Patience, patience!"

"Is this the name of the cake?" she continued to stare at him in total incomprehension.

"The marzipan is needed as a decoration. I have a brilliant idea!"

Cecily Clumsy was almost intoxicated by the excitement.

"What fun!" she gave a loud, amused chuckle.

When Cecily returned with the marzipan, Peter revealed his plan to her.

The little vole had taken inspiration from his morning escapade: he wanted to make a cake with an edible marzipan decoration on top instead of a real prickly pine twig.

Cecily mixed the ingredients for the sponge cake, and a few minutes later the mixture was in the oven and quickly baked. When the cake had cooled to room temperature, it was cut in half and filled with chocolate orange cream, then cut into slices.

A twig decoration made from marzipan was laid on the top of each slice. As a finishing touch, with a tiny sieve Peter sprinkled some powdered sugar on top of each slice of the cake, so it looked like snowflakes. When Cecily had finished thanking him profusely, Peter broke into a run, as he still had plenty to do.

The mayor angrily told Peter off for arriving for the cake contest at the very last moment.

"Where have you been? I have been looking for you everywhere!"

"Patience, patience! Everyone is in the right place now, so we can start the contest!" Peter interrupted the mayor firmly, and took his place on the stage.

Peter's confident manner left the mayor speechless. A buzz of excitement went through the audience as he went on the stage, where the jury's table was placed. A young mouse lady pressed the list with the names of the contestants into Peter's hand and he called them one by one, intentionally leaving Cecily to the end.

Each contestant came to the jury's table to present his or her work. The committee tasted and hummed and hawed before evaluating each item. Finally, Cecily's turn had come.

"Cecily Clumsy," Peter called her name loudly.

The charming Cecily appeared in her tiny stilettos with a tray in her hand. She leapt onto the stage like a chamois and showed her sponge cake to the members of the jury, proud and happy.

"We have already seen this cake!" one of the mouse ladies hissed, peering at Cecily through her spectacles.

"No, not like this," Cecily retorted. "Just taste it, please! Even the decoration is edible!"

The soft warm cake almost melted in the mouths of the judges.

"Can I keep the decoration? I can take it home, can't I?" asked one of the judges.

"And what is the name of this fantastic wonder?" one of the judges asked with interest.

Cecily was struck dumb. 'The name of the cake! I completely forgot about that!' she thought. The mouse lady looked at Peter Vole in despair.

However, the little vole heroically fought the difficult situation. "Patience is the name of the cake."

"Patience? What a weird name for a cake!" one of the members of the jury said in amazement.

"The reason for this name is that it took a lot of patience to make it. Patience is the main flavour of everything!" the little vole said very proudly.

The jury soon made its decision. The winner of the contest was Cecily Clumsy. This delighted many of the townspeople, especially her friends. It also taught everybody an important lesson: patience is the road to a better life. This moral was engraved in Peter's memory forever as he was reminded of it every time he thought of this most delicious Christmas cake.

CPSIA information can be obtained
at www.ICGtesting.com
Printed in the USA
LVHW071540300922
729671LV00015B/771